WELCOME TO SLEEPYTOWN

WELCOME TO
SLEEPYTOWN

MARK A. RANDALL

WELCOME TO SLEEPYTOWN
Written and Illustrated by Mark A. Randall

www.welcometosleepytown.com
www.myspace.com/welcometosleepytown

Manufactured in the United States of America

First printing: June 2009
Wordclay Publishing

ISBN: 978-1-6048-1648-8 (sc)

For July

CONTENTS

WELCOME TO SLEEPYTOWN

Welcome from the Mayor

The first thing you notice upon entering Sleepytown is how relaxed and at ease you feel. The pioneers experienced that same thing when they arrived here in the early 1800s. This charming little town nestled comfortably in the heart of the Midwest is a place far away from the hustle and bustle of big city life.

It's a place where the people are friendly, and everyone knows their neighbors. There's a great sense of community pride in our many historic buildings, homes, and neighborhoods. The centerpiece of town is the Davenport County Courthouse, which prominently anchors the main street district. All our businesses are locally owned and include a newspaper, flower shop, hardware store, bakery, bookstore, and a variety of antique stores, just to name a few.

Established in 1835, the population stands at 2,693 and increases to nearly 3,000 during any number of the town's annual festivities. A few examples are the Ladies Auxiliary Day of Schnecken social gathering; the Fourth of July All-Star-Spangled Spectacular, which includes food, fun, and a stunning fireworks display presented by the Eldeberry Sisters; and the ever-popular Squirrel Days held in the fall.

Sleepytown also has a rich history of folk tales and local legends. From the pioneers' first arrival to the present, town records are filled with reports of bizarre creatures and odd encounters. Rather than shunning this reputation, however, Sleepytown embraces it. Of course, this means you might spot the widow Jenkins washing her clothes (and herself) in the square fountain. Just don't make direct eye contact, and you'll be fine.

Enjoy your visit.
Walter Weshley

"One of the first businesses here in town caused quite an uproar. I guess folks just didn't share shop owner Merle Dean's passion for boudoir britches and whatnot."

-Lyndon Allspice

HISTORY OF SLEEPYTOWN

They Call Me Mr. Tibbs

The town was given its name by Beauregard Roscoe Tibbs, founding father and one of the area's early settlers. Beauregard had eagerly volunteered to lead a small group of settlers west from Virginia in search of new land. He was highly regarded among his peers as the consummate outdoorsman. An expert in tracking, fishing, and hunting, he had once fought off two angry elk with nothing more than a shoehorn for defense. Despite his many talents and heroics, however, this man held a deep, dark secret. It's not something you're likely to find in the history books, but Beauregard spent his entire life a habitual thumbsucker. Only coming to light after both he and his wife had passed, private journal entries show a man at odds with his inner demons. Abandoned as an infant and raised by vagabonds, the only comfort Beauregard ever found was sucking his thumb while clinging to his favorite blanket. He was able to hide the thumbsucking from public view, but people would often question why a grown man would carry around an old, tattered quilt. Beauregard explained this by saying he was simply a cold-natured person.

Today, despite this posthumous discovery, Beauregard is still regarded as a local legend and the individual who gave the town its name so many years ago. Casting his first gaze upon the picturesque landscape, he declared, "This view makes me sleepy...oh so sleepy."

Porcine Pranksters

Despite their initial love for the land, life for the early pioneers was a constant struggle against disease, wildlife, and the Native American population. If that wasn't enough, the settlers also dealt with matters of a more bizarre nature. Historical records are filled with all sorts of strange and eerie tales: tales of ghosts, lake monsters, winged creatures, and beings from the stars. There are also numerous stories of trolls and goblins causing mischief. It's almost certain the settlers encountered things they didn't know how to explain properly. It's also possible that they were absolutely right in their accounts.

For example, take this story by pioneer Wilberforce Beardsley. Certain aspects are a bit sketchy, but the gist of his account is intact. Beardsley writes,

> "It was our second evening camped in this heavenly wonderland when we were startled by a terrifying sound. A short, squat pig-of-a-man stood before us. His feet were cloven like that of a goat, and his belly protruded from beneath his primitive attire. He communicated through a series of guttural growls, grunts, and obscene hand gestures. We ascertained from the minute stranger that he wanted us to follow him as he made a lewd gesture toward a nearby hill. Beauregard, several other men, and I warily accepted to accompany the creature to a ramshackle dwelling. There we found a group of similar creatures huddled around a campfire drinking from an animal skin flask. It was then... *undecipherable*... as we awoke the next morning to find ourselves stripped of our clothing and covered head to toe in manure and feathers. In the distance, we could hear the raucous laughter of our porcine neighbors."

Birdie Bill Chamberlain

Another hero from Sleepytown's past who made a name for himself in the late 1800s was Birdie Bill Chamberlain. Birdie Bill was the sheriff of Sleepytown during the days of lawlessness after the Civil War. At first glance, Birdie was not the typical lawman. He stood just a whisker over four feet tall and had the odd ability to communicate with all manner of fowl, but history would prove he was the right man for the time.

Sleepytown certainly didn't have the rough reputation of towns like Deadwood or Dodge City, but it did see its fair share of outlaws and desperadoes pass through. A few of note include Miss Elly Anos and her gang, The Lamb Fry Kid, Lilly Wushbacker, and Johnny "One-Ball" McAllister, whose confrontation with Birdie was bizarre, to say the least.

After being refused at the local saloon, Johnny began shooting the place up. Birdie stepped in to stop him but was momentarily distracted and knocked out cold. When Birdie regained consciousness, he looked around and came to the horrific realization that he was hogtied to the bottom of a stagecoach. Suddenly, Johnny slapped the horses sending them into a rampaging frenzy. It was over an hour later when the townsfolk found Birdie beaten and bruised near the livery barn. With blood in his eyes, he slowly hobbled back to the saloon where Johnny sat drinking and shot him squarely in the knapsack.

Bouffant Brothers Gone Wild

Clarence and Drayton Bouffant were two of the wildest, most ornery jokesters you would ever run across. Never evil or mean-spirited, they were simply unable to pass up a good time.

Bringing Up Bouffant

The brothers were born in the late 1800s and raised by their Grandfather, "Grampa" Boutris Bouffant. It's not known exactly what happened to the boys' parents, but Grampa always claimed they had been carried off by a giant thunderbird named Nanumchuk while out gathering firewood. Stranger things have happened.

Grampa certainly had his hands full with the two boys. When they were young, they helped with the day-to-day chores on the farm, but as they grew older it was all Grampa could do to keep them focused on their work. They would often just drop what they were doing to wrestle with a bull, tie a snake into knots, or play a game of "ferret in the trousers." That was short-lived, however, when Clarence was bitten in the unmentionables. It was said he walked with a slight limp the rest of his life.

Another close call for Clarence came when he was nearly mauled to death after he mistook a bobcat for his brother. He saw what he thought was Drayton sleeping under a shade tree and, as usual, decided to pull a prank on him. He carefully snuck up as close as he could, let out an Indian war cry, and leapt onto its back. It took less than a second for him to realize he had made a terrible mistake. The scene was a frenzy of teeth and claws as the bobcat handled Clarence like a whiskey-soaked rag doll. Suddenly, shots rang out. As Drayton prepared to fire again, the beast let go of Clarence and retreated to the woods. With his clothes in tatters, a wobbly Clarence simply brushed himself off and let out a resounding belly laugh!

No West for the Wicked

During their late teens, the boys began to grow restless and yearned to escape the confines of their small town. They wanted to strike out on their own, away from their grandfather, and experience what the rest of the country had to offer. So with barely enough sense between the two of them, they headed West in search of adventure.

The boys' first taste of freedom came when they applied for jobs as horse wranglers on a cattle drive. The days were long and the work grueling, or so the trail boss said, but Clarence and Drayton thought it sounded like fun. Two days later, under the hot Texas sun, the boys had had enough. That night they got the cook drunk, hijacked the chuck wagon, and left the herd behind. The wagon was found the next day wrecked and completely emptied of its contents.

In Kansas, they were nearly lynched when they were caught impersonating members of the clergy. The boys had stolen some priest robes and convinced a group of young ladies to accompany them to a nearby pond. They were just beginning the "baptism" when an angry mob of locals found them. Clarence and Drayton barely escaped with their sacraments intact. Eventually, they were run out of one state too many and decided to hightail it back home.

And Grampa Makes Three

Arriving back in Sleepytown, Clarence and Drayton were met by the town doctor. He had sad news. Grampa Boutris' heart was failing, and he wasn't expected to live much longer. The boys were in shock. Heading to the farm, they were determined to put up a brave front, but it wasn't necessary. Upon seeing the two, Grampa sprang from his bed to give them each a homecoming hug.

Over the next few weeks, Clarence and Drayton, with Grampa Boutris by their side, carried on with wild abandon. It was all Sheriff Birdie Bill could do to keep up with them and their shenanigans. He had enough trouble dealing with the influx of riff-raff and hooligans that were trying to make Sleepytown their home. He kept a close eye on the trio but notes in his journal, "they were behaving more like schoolchildren than ruffians." He goes on to write, "as long as their actions remain harmless, I will turn a blind eye to their juvenile activity."

Sadly, just a few days after an unfortunate incident involving donkey races, a wedding cake, and the bride-to-be, Grampa passed away quietly in his sleep. He was laid to rest beneath a grove of trees just on the edge of his farm. As for Clarence and Drayton, amazingly, they went on to live a long life, full of mischief, never straying far from the small farm on which they grew up. And when they passed away, they were laid under the same grove of trees, with Grampa separating them, of course.

Heel to the Chief

A five-year-old dog named Charlie held the office of mayor (if only for a brief moment) during the elections of 1880. Charlie's owner ran him as a write-in candidate to show his disapproval with the choice of the other two parties. Other citizens soon rallied around Charlie, and on Election Day he was elected mayor of Sleepytown in a sweeping victory. His tenure would be short-lived, however, when on inauguration day he was seen licking himself in public.

The Great Squirrel Uprising of 1893

Perhaps the most memorable event in Sleepytown's history occurred in 1893. Frances McFarland had opened a small bakery, and business was booming. People were coming from miles around to purchase her homemade cookies, muffins, and pies. One of the main ingredients in her baking were nuts gathered from the nearby farms. At first there was no problem because the surrounding land was plentiful. But soon the nut supply began to dwindle, and that's when the trouble started....

As the sun came up on the morning of October 3, 1893, nothing seemed out of the ordinary in the small town. Suddenly, the sound of thunder arose, and in the distance a gray cloud appeared. As it moved closer, the people could hear a deafening chatter unlike anything heard before. It was a horde of squirrels, and they were mad as hell. Chaos erupted as the town was besieged by the frenzy of bushy tails and gnashing teeth. Men shuddered, women fainted, and children cried. People were forced indoors afraid to be left alone on the streets. As one eyewitness recounted, "Lord amighty! Those little, furry sumbitches were everywhere! They were even in our outhouse, for God's sake! It was madness, I tell you! MADNESS!"

After three days of utter pandemonium, local farmer and Civil War hero Lucious Grainger stepped forward to try to end the siege. Followed by hordes of the bushy-tailed terrors, Lucious led the squirrels off to an open pasture on the outskirts of town. As the townsfolk peered out of their homes and businesses, they feared they would never see their friend alive again. After what seemed like hours, Lucious returned alone to deliver a warning to the townspeople. The message was quite succinct, "Keep your hands off our nuts!" Lucious never divulged how he came up with this information, but from that day forward there has been peaceful coexistence between man and squirrel in Sleepytown. In 1908, the town council approved the building of a statue on the courthouse lawn to commemorate the event. A small inscription reads, "To make amends to our furry friends, the people of Sleepytown vow never again to lay a finger on the nuts of our neighbors."

"On a hot summer evening, we like to walk down to the Frosty Freezy. I usually get a twist cone, and my cow Buttercup gets the rainbow sundae with lots of sprinkles."

-Hoyt Sealbatt

LIFE IN SLEEPYTOWN

Grizzle Lee's Mini-Mart and Rattlesnake Petting Park

If you're hot and thirsty and running low on gas, you'll want to stop at Grizzle Lee's Mini-Mart and Rattlesnake Petting Park on old US 47. Rattlers, you ask? You heard right. Back behind the store is the snake park with hundreds of live rattlers for viewing and handling. The featured attraction is the "Hanging Gardens" where snakes dangle overhead in an ivy-covered structure. For the convenience of the visitors, the first-aid station is located at the garden's entrance.

Asked what would possess anyone to combine these two disparate ideas, Grady "Grizzle" Lee responds, "I used to be a truck driver and found the road could be a cold and lonely place. One day I got myself a pet snake, and he became my traveling buddy and confidant. To pass the time, we'd talk about all sorts of things, and the idea for this came up. Before you know it, I was buying this place and hauling in snakes by the truckload!"

One aspect of the business that has gained some widespread popularity is Grizzle Lee's traveling companion and store mascot, Teddie the Rattlesnake. His image graces everything from the logo and advertisements to soft drink cups and merchandising of all kinds. He has become a local celebrity.

"Teddie is one of a kind," Grady says. "He puts up with all the promotional appearances and autograph seekers better than I would. He doesn't ask for much except for time off every other Saturday to go visit his son, Teddie Jr. He's a true professional."

Blue Belly

Despite the fact that Sleepytown hosts numerous events a year, the annual Blue Belly Festival stands out as being a bit more colorful than the others.

Chairman Sassy Carlysle explains how the festival got started, "The original organizers were out camping and drinking one fall evening when, I guess, they got bored. Someone brought out a can of blue paint, and before you know it, everyone was running around acting like idiots and painting their stomachs. I'm not really sure how, but for some reason a festival evolved from that, and we've been celebrating it for the past 25 years."

Somewhere along the way the festival changed from a rather decadent affair into a strictly family-friendly event. It runs for three days and includes a parade, fish fry, kiddie rides, entertainment, and music. There's even a Mr. and Mrs. Blue Belly chosen to hold the crown for one year.

The festival isn't without controversy, however. Today the festival has all but banned the practice that gave it its name. The town forbids painting of any kind, and instead attendees are only allowed to wear t-shirts with blue silk-screened designs.

Sassy says, "We had to bar the use of actual paint because people were going around town painting everything but their bellies. It really got out of control. Hardcore purists said they were trying to return the festival to its roots, but if you ask me it was just the corn liquor doing the talking. It got so bad that people were even painting their pets. And let me tell you, it's not easy to wash blue paint out of cat fur!"

Whiskers

Located just three miles west of Sleepytown on Tobler Road stands the Harvest Moon Flea Market and Lunch Wagon. The market has six tents of stalls containing a wide variety of items to suit any need.

Margaret DeCicco, or "Whiskers" as she is called by the townsfolk, has owned and operated the market for the past eight years. She started it in 1999 after her bid for sanitation commissioner fell through.

"I decided to open this up once I realized my political dreams were over. Anyway, besides running the place, I've got two tables full of stuff. Most of it came outta my own trailer, but every once in a while I find something along the road or visit the dumpsters behind the local strip mall. Those are some high-quality items even if they are missing parts. My daughter Lulu usually comes with me if she's not in school. She's a little livewire who's always finding stuff at the other tables and wanting me to buy it for her. Just yesterday she wanted $2.00 to buy a bucket of old corroded batteries. I swear, sometimes that girl's got the brains God gave a piss ant."

The other attraction at the market is the lunch wagon, which features whatever Whiskers might have in her pantry on any given day.

"Yeah, I do it all around here. Every morning I get up and make nine or ten baloney sandwiches. Sometimes I'll throw on some cheese, but it really just depends. Then I'll fill some baggies with chips or crackers, put 'em all in a brown bag, and call it done. It started out as a way to make some extra money, but the fact is I hardly sell any. Lulu and me usually end up eating most of them anyway."

Ol' Snookie's

If you're a visitor to Sleepytown and looking for a unique dining experience, make sure to check out Ol' Snookie's Seafood and Fun. What makes Snookie's so unusual is the fact that the restaurant is actually onboard an old riverboat dry-docked some five miles from the nearest waterway. Old-timers claim it was shipwrecked here during the great flood of 1915 when it rained for twelve days straight. After the waters receded, no one claimed the craft, and it simply became a permanent fixture in town.

Decades later, as Sleepytown grew and businesses began springing up, the town council was faced with a dilemma. What should be done with the wayward watercraft? That's when long-time resident Lou "Snookie" Fellers stepped in.

"Believe you me, this wasn't the first thing I had in here. My first business was a ladies clothing store, but to tell you the truth, I don't know nothin' about fashion. That was all my wife's idea. Plus, the name "Fellers Boutique" kinda gave people the wrong impression, if you know what I mean. Then I tried getting into the discount market and ended up selling all sorts of things. It was called "Lou's Knives, Leather, Swimwear, and Fudge Emporium." That lasted a little over a year. Nothing I did seemed to work. I thought at first it was what I was trying to sell, but then I looked at the property. It's a boat, for God's sake! I realized people don't want to come aboard a boat to try on fancy clothes and buy fudge. That's when it hit me to open a seafood restaurant."

Today Ol' Snookie's is considered a landmark in Sleepytown. Since opening in 1978, it has drawn customers from far and wide for its great food, fun atmosphere, and of course, its unique exterior. "Once I hit on the seafood angle, things just clicked," says Lou. "Everything's been fine since. Oh, except for the issue with Dixieland Jazz music, but we don't play that anymore."

Claudia Brandishire and her husband Jim are frequent patrons to Snookie's. Claudia says, "We love it here. We don't get out of town much, but when we're here it's like we're on vacation or something. We usually come on Thursdays for the walleye and hushpuppies special. It's a good deal 'cause you get a side of coleslaw, fries, and your drink for $6.95. But if it's a real special occasion, we might get Ol' Snookie's All-You-Can-Eat Platter. It's got fish planks, salmon patties, lobster bites, crab cakes, hushpuppies, and clam balls! Jim just can't say no to the clam balls!"

Pet Pageants

At 83 years of age, you might think retired farmer Bob "Bobby" Bobson would be spending his twilight years taking it easy. But for the past five years, he has been part of the exciting world of pet pageants. From his farm just outside of town, Bobby teaches the young and old alike the tricks of the pet pageant trade. Four-legged students and their owners learn about stage presence, beauty, attire (dress for success), and costuming. There's even a stage inside the barn for mock competitions.

Bobby explains how it all started, "Well, one day I was out feeding the chickens. I don't know why, but I wondered what it would be like to dress 'em up in costume. I took this little feller I had named Frenchie and put a tiny cowboy hat and vest on him. He looked a riot! He was strutting around like he owned the place. My

neighbor came by and said I should enter him in the Davenport County Fair Pet Pageant, so one month later I did. And do you know what? He won first place in the costuming division! I knew right then and there that's what we should be doing. We worked the pageant circuit for quite a few years until I noticed a change in Frenchie. He was getting cranky and just wasn't enjoying it as much as he once had. That's when he decided to retire, and I decided to start teaching these classes."

Despite the growing popularity of pet pageants, they do have their detractors. Critics say animals shouldn't be forced to be paraded around like, well, animals. They also claim they are unnecessarily subjected to wearing ill-fitting clothing or having to endure harsh practice conditions.

"It's too much for an animal to take," says Sandy Shoffy. "I've seen a pig forced to sit through an hour-long make-up session which included rouge and fake eyelashes! That same pig even received a full-body massage!"

But owners disagree with the criticism. They say the pageants work to instill confidence and a sense of achievement in the animal whether they come in first or last. Though they admit the sight of animals wearing clothes is pretty funny.

"Despite all the hard work you put into training and character building," says Bobby, "the truth is, you're not going to score any points with the judges if your chicken doesn't look good in his little tuxedo."

Schnieppschaub

Just on the outskirts of town lives a family well-known in these parts. Seven sisters, all of whom are entertainers, have been trying to make it big for the past 70 years. Despite setback after embarrassing setback, they're a determined bunch spurred on by family matriarch, Momma Schnieppschaub.

As you approach the Schnieppschaub homestead, you hear what sounds like an animal with its foot caught in a trap. The noise is quite unsettling, and you begin to wonder if someone or something is being tortured. Once inside, however, you see the source of the commotion. The tiny living room is crowded with women: some are playing piano, guitar, and banjo; some are singing, dancing, and performing; and one is frantically scribbling away at the coffee table with a crayon. Momma Schnieppschaub sits quietly amidst the chaos. Now ninety years old, her snowball white hair is disheveled, and her face and hands are withered from the years. She seems oblivious to the whirlwind around her. As the noisy crowd moves outdoors, Momma finally has a moment of peace and begins to speak about her brood.

"My girls have always been a rambunctious bunch, but they act as if they're still in short pants, not grown women. Now that they all live here again, it's like this 24 hours a day!

"All the girls...well, most of them anyway, at one time or another, tried leaving to join the outside world. One by one, though, they started coming back whether it was from lousy jobs, failed marriages, or the dozen or so rejections by the Rockettes.

"They're all artists and performers, you see. Lydia is my youngest. She's always painting or drawing. It's as if the paper can't contain her creativity. That's why I just let her go ahead and scribble all over the furniture. In a few days, they'll all be a different color anyway. The twins, Caroline and Gwendoline, are the song and dance duo. They've been doing this since they were in diapers, and just look at them today- still entertaining, still in diapers. All the girls are hams when it comes to performing, but Tina really has the acting bug. She's always pestering her sisters to help with her plays.

"I remember once during their performance of 'Gone with the Wind' the girls were re-enacting the burning of Atlanta, and Tina set fire to the sofa. I'll bet it took three weeks to get the smell out of the house!

"Loretta, Josie, and Peggy are the musicians in the family. They learned to play the guitar and banjo all by themselves. The fact is when they play it sounds like three tomcats scratching and clawing at..."

Suddenly Momma is interrupted as the screen door swings open, and the women begin to pile back inside, their voices rising to a deafening crescendo.

As she watches her kids, a tear comes to her eye. "God bless them, they try. They surely do try, but none of them's got the least bit of talent. Not a one. Of course, I don't tell them that. It's my fault, I guess. I encouraged them every step of the way. Don't get me wrong. I love all my kids dearly. I do. But it's like beating a dead horse. After seventy years of this, the girls just need to hang it up. I need a break too, you know? Momma needs some quiet time. And if I never hear another hymn as long as I live, it won't be soon enough."

As if on cue, the girls launch into a rousing version of "I've Got the Joy, Joy, Joy, Joy Down in my Heart." Momma buries her head in her hands and mutters, "Oh, dear sweet Lord in Heaven. Take me now."

Tit for Tat

One of the town's longest-running social clubs is the Victory Belles, a group of over fifties who meet once every three weeks. Since the club's inception in 1951, the group has done its fair share of baking, quilting, crafting, event planning, and volunteering. But one new activity has been taking up a lot of the members' time recently: tattooing.

It began harmlessly enough when club treasurer Virginia Tutwiler bragged about her new tattoo. She had taken a trip to the big city and on a whim decided to get a small butterfly for her ankle. The other ladies were shocked at first, but then good ol' jealous rivalry set in. Not to be outdone, other members began getting tattoos- each one a bit bigger and more prominently displayed than the next.

Now, 2 years and nearly 30 tattoos later, it seems the "competition" may be wildly out of control. When asked, 78-year-old Margaret Lovejoy responds, "I've got three right now, and I'm working on a fourth. My first was a playful kitty on my shoulder, but then Alice had to go and get an American eagle on her back. Since then, I've added a cute Calico cat to my wrist and a Maine Coon to my thigh."

And what do their husbands, children, and the rest of the community think of the body art? "Well, both of my grown kids say I'm out of my ever-lovin' mind. They're ready to have me put away. Once in awhile when you're out and about, you get someone giving you dirty looks, but at my age I could care less. I think I look pretty darn good with these. Like this one. I really like the way this kitty's whiskers hide my varicose veins."

Deliver Us from Evil

It's a hot summer day when you hear a faint sound in the distance. As it grows louder, you begin to make out the familiar strands of carnival music. Suddenly it hits you! It's the ice cream man, and you scramble to gather up whatever loose change you can find. Rushing to the street, money in hand, your excitement suddenly turns to horror. Instead of a brightly-colored van full of tasty frozen treats, it's a dirty brown leisure van stinking of diesel and formaldehyde. If you're a long-time resident of Sleepytown, you know all about Forrest Charboneu's Traveling Taxidermy Showroom and Delivery. To those unfamiliar, seeing Forrest drive into your cul-de-sac can be quite a shock!

It all started in 2005 while Forrest worked for the county highway department. He had only been on the job a few months when he was caught taking home unauthorized road kill. Forrest claimed he had ordered a home taxidermy course and simply needed specimens on which to practice. His excuse didn't go over too well with his bosses, however, and he was fired on the spot.

Suddenly jobless, Forrest jumped headfirst into learning the taxidermy trade. During the day, he slaved away inside his cramped garage apartment working with scavenged remains found the night before. Oftentimes he was forced to combine different animal parts, resulting in what some would later describe as "freakish oddities better left to a horror movie than displayed in someone's home." Finally, after just four short weeks, Forrest was ready to show off the fruits of his labor. He began converting his old van into a traveling showroom. He packed it with wall-to-wall critters and even installed a loudspeaker so he could pipe out music. With everything in place, Forrest set out into an unsuspecting world.

Immediately, Forrest's sculptures were met with public disgust. He had unwisely decided to go door-to-door and began dropping in at public functions unannounced. People all over town started to complain of being unceremoniously accosted by Forrest toting one of his horrific pieces. A general feeling of uneasiness quickly took hold of Sleepytown. Soon the complaints found their way to the town council who surprisingly voted in favor of Forrest, albeit with a minor stipulation: they ruled that as long as he kept his figures inside the truck and out of public view, he could continue.

Unfortunately, after three years, Forrest has had little success selling his creations. Folks who showed the slightest interest in his work only did so out of a sense of curiosity, and there weren't many of them to begin with. Now desperate and perhaps slightly affected by the taxidermy chemicals, Forrest has started flaunting the law that prohibited him from keeping his creatures out of sight.

Councilwoman Cora May Wooley responds, "Yes, we understand Forrest has been showing his goods again in public. We actually just received a call saying he had crashed a Victory Belles luncheon over at Community Hall. The caller said he staggered into the place and appeared unwell. He was clutching several of his pieces and began screaming, 'I've got me a real perty one. Would you like to touch it?' Unfortunately for him, those Victory Belle gals are a tough bunch. I guess they beat the tar out of him pretty good. The caller said that after they got through with him, he looked almost as bad as that stuff he's been peddling."

"We came upon the creature rummaging through our coolers. It had piercing red eyes and what looked like white cupcake frosting around its mouth."

-Linda Mango

SPOOKY SLEEPYTOWN

UFOS &
ALIENS

Guess Who's Coming to Dinner?

Mysterious reports involving UFOs and little green men have been around these parts since the mid-1800s. The first mention of these otherworldly visitors can be found in the journal of Reverend Ambrose Jacoby. He notes that during a summer revival picnic the congregation was visited by strange beings from the sky. After descending from the heavens in an "illuminated sphere," three small green men emerged and joined in the day-long festivities. Then as night fell, they boarded their craft and rose back into the sky. Despite their freakish appearance and unintelligible language, Reverend Jacoby writes that a good time was had by all. However, he does mention that following the alien's departure, the collection plate containing a sum of $4.35 was reported missing.

Being Neighborly

Eighty-one-year-old Lydia Boujele claims that for the past two years she has been visited by the proverbial little green men from outer space. According to Lydia, this is all just part of her normal everyday life in the Squirrel's Nest Trailer Park Community.

"I'm a real night owl. One evening I was sitting here at my card table working on a new puzzle; it was a real pretty one with a running stream and saw mill. All of a sudden, the whole trailer started shaking like a freight train was coming right through the living room. It darn near bounced my puzzle on the floor! I got up and looked outside, but it was too dark, and I wasn't about to go outside at that time of night. I just decided to go to bed. That's when there was a knock at my door. Lord only knows why I opened it, but I did. And there, standing in the pouring rain, were three of the cutest little aliens you would ever meet. I could tell right away that's what they were 'cause I watch those shows on TV. They looked so helpless, and they were cold and shivering, so I invited them in. It took us a little while to get acquainted because they're real animated and talk really fast in a high squeaky voice. You know, like on those old chipmunk records. But once the awkwardness was out of the way, we had a nice visit. After four hours of showing them my puzzles and looking through old photo albums, I got the feeling they were tired, so I made them all a nice comfy spot on the floor and said goodnight. When I woke up, the aliens were gone, and my puzzle was finished.

"I thought that might be the last I'd see of them, but every couple of weeks they show up out of the blue. When they come over, we do all sorts of things. We spend the night watching TV or playing games. What they really like to do is gossip. They're always telling me about so-and-so across the way. I'm not sure how they know all this stuff, but they've got some goods on people, I can tell you!

"Folks have asked if I think they mean me any harm. My answer is a definite 'No.' They've never so much as laid their little three-fingered hands on me. People also ask if I know why the aliens are here. I've tried to ask them that myself, and each time I do, they get a little snippy with me. From what I've been able to gather, they wrecked their space car pretty good. It's still around here in the woods somewhere, but it's all busted up. Now they're stuck waiting on replacement parts or someone to come get them. I don't know. It's a touchy subject."

No Fly Zone

Over the years, more strange sightings and visitors have been reported, but it wasn't until the summer of 1995 that the aliens decided to ratchet up the excitement around Sleepytown. That's when two mysterious crop formations appeared in the fields of local farmer Eustes Ollister. But all was not well. As the circles popped up, so did the tourists. Every day for three weeks straight, people would arrive with their cameras and equipment scouring the countryside. Paying no heed to Mr. Ollister's no trespassing signs, they trampled what little crop he had left to get a closer look at the so-called "marvels of alien intelligence."

Growing tired of the endless parade of people, Euestes thought up a plan to get rid of the problem once and for all. Working throughout the night, he decided to send his own special message to the aliens and the nosy sightseers. At 8:00 a.m. the buses started to arrive as usual, but as the visitors began entering the fields, they noticed something peculiar in the air. Euestes had carefully lined both circles with pungent manure fertilizer.

People were aghast! Why would he do such a thing? As expected, the buses packed up, and the people left in droves never to return.

Defending his actions, Eustes explains, "I put up with all the nonsense as long as I could. I'm not really against UFOs and such. There might be something to it. What I am against are the idiots who swarmed around my farm likes flies on a rib roast."

Outhouse of Body Experience

Encounters with extraterrestrial intelligence can occur any time and any place. Such is the case involving Mervis Delroy, a local farmer who had an unusual experience several years ago. Mervis explains the incident,

"It was a real cool fall night, and I was out doin' my business. All of a sudden there was this real bright light inside the outhouse. It was blindin' me it was so bright! I started fumblin' around tryin' to pull up my britches when this strange feelin' came over me. It was almost like I was bein' wrapped up in a warm, fuzzy blanket. I closed my eyes for a second, and when I opened them, I wasn't in the outhouse anymore. I was in a big, shiny room surrounded by these odd-lookin' fellas. They had big heads and great big eyes, and it looked like they only had three fingers. I think there were six or seven of them, and one by one they all took turns proddin' and pokin' at me for what seemed forever. Actually, now that I think about it, they did have three fingers. Anyway, one of them came over to me and started talkin' some sort of jibber-jabber. I couldn't understand a damn thing he was saying, so I looked that ugly little sucker in the eye and yelled as loud as I could, 'I-don't-un-der-stand-you!' And then I'll be damned, it was just like someone flipped a switch. All of a sudden, I could hear words I knew- not that I understood what he was sayin'. He rattled on and on and about God knows what. There was somethin' about past visits and aliens in the government and the end of the world or some such nonsense. I'm not really sure what all he said 'cause I started to get that warm feelin' again, and the next thing I know I'm face down in my back yard. I tried openin' my eyes, but they were burnin' real bad- so were my buttocks for some reason. There was smoke everywhere. I finally got my eyes open and looked over to see the outhouse in flames. All I could think was, sonuvabitch! There goes my magazine collection down the crapper!"

PARANORMAL INVESTIGATORS

Hell Toupee

In a town with as many strange goings-on as Sleepytown, it only makes sense to have someone around who knows a thing or two about the supernatural. Meet two such people: Fritz and Betty Shanks, ghost hunters and tour guides. They first came for a visit in 2003 after hearing about the odd occurrences through friends. Just minutes after arriving, Fritz, who is a psychic, noticed something unusual.

"Well, my mustache started twitching, which is what happens when I'm near ghostly activity. I've often had this tingling sensation in my body, but I never knew what it was. It wasn't until I grew this mustache that the tingling manifested itself in my whiskers."

What makes Betty tingle, you ask? It's probably one of her many pieces of ghost-detecting equipment. Although not psychic herself, she is able to locate spirits through temperature changes, abnormal energy fields, and E.V.P. (electronic voice phenomena).

Now four years after that first visit, the Shanks are Sleepytown's resident ghost hunting duo. Operating out of a second-story office on the town square, their caseload is overflowing. They've investigated everything from haunted houses to haunted outhouses and just about everything in between. They've even investigated a haunted toupee.

"Oh boy. That was one of our first cases, and it didn't turn out well at all," Betty recounts. "This nice elderly gentleman claimed there was something peculiar about his toupee, and he wanted us to come check it out. Well, we had just arrived at the man's house and started setting up our equipment when I looked up to see Fritz suddenly pounce on this poor man's wig. To this day he swears it flinched, but regardless, it was completely destroyed. The old man took it better than expected, although he did ask we pay $45.00 for a new hairpiece. It's not exactly how you want to conduct yourselves during an investigation. For all his talents, bless his heart, Fritz is a bit of a weenie."

Spooky Tours

Despite their full workload of ghostly investigations, Fritz and Betty have started yet another paranormal venture. A year ago they decided to offer the Sleepytown Ghost Tours so the general public could experience and visit some of the town's spooky and mysterious places. Currently, the tour runs Friday and Saturday nights beginning in the summer and running through Halloween.

Betty describes the tour, "We're slowly building up a nice word-of-mouth. Right now I would say the majority of our attendees are from outside Sleepytown. Most of the people here are so accustomed to the strangeness that they don't need to pay for a guided tour. I can understand that. The tour itself runs about two hours and covers approximately 12 miles of the town and surrounding area. A few of the locations we visit are way out in the boondocks like Robey Lake and Hedley Hollow. Fritz isn't the best driver in the world, so sometimes his driving is scarier than the places we visit!"

Asked if they have ever encountered anything while on the tour, Betty replies, "We've had a few sightings. There have been some unexplainable lights in the sky, and we've caught some ghostly forms on camera. One night we thought we saw the elusive flying lizard man that is said to haunt the old reservoir, but it turned out to be that nitwit Fred Jesse peeing off the lookout platform."

Hall Aflame

"Fritz and I had been asked to attend a Christmas Eve Candlelight Service at the Sleepy Valley Chapel. The little rustic church was over 100 years old and had withstood every conceivable disaster God could throw its way including flood, tornadoes, and a fire that almost took down the historic structure.

"As the service progressed, the pastor asked everyone to stand for the lighting of the candles. Slowly and solemnly the congregation filed to the front of the altar to take their own candle. Soon the walls of the tiny church were lined by the soft glow as we stood in silence. A few moments passed, and we all began singing 'Silent Night.' We were halfway through the second verse when I noticed an unusual smell. I looked over at Fritz, and there he stood oblivious to the fact that his mustache was on fire. As I leaned in to tell him, he suddenly realized what was happening and began squealing like a schoolgirl. I could hear the minister yelling from the pulpit, 'Stop, drop, and roll! Stop, drop, and roll!' As Fritz finally began to calm down, I could see that he was ok. More importantly, his mustache looked unharmed. Only the tips had been singed.

"A few weeks later, everything was back to normal as Fritz and I investigated yet another location. As I watched my husband go about his work, I started to think back to the events of Christmas Eve. A cold chill suddenly shot through me. I had seen Fritz in peril before, but something about that night and that experience changed me forever. I had to make a decision that from now on open flames were definitely off-limits to Fritz. After all, someone's got to look out for that cash cow of ours."

Do You Hear What I Hear?

"One of our most promising (but ultimately disappointing) investigations was at Foley Manor. Here in Sleepytown it's the quintessential haunted house. It's deserted, dilapidated, and there are numerous reports of paranormal activity. The house has an interesting history. A young girl was engaged to be married, and every day her fiancé would come to call, bringing with him a single red rose. One day, however, the fiancé did not arrive. It was later discovered he had fallen into an open well near the back of the home. Found on the edge of the well was a single red rose. With her heart broken, the girl took her own life by drinking arsenic. She was found in her upstairs bedroom.

"Since then people have experienced all sorts of activity inside and outside the home. The last family to live there left after only a week. They said they were kept awake almost nightly by the sound of footsteps and odd voices. They also reported seeing a dark shape around the spot of the old well. The house has been vacant now for nearly a year, the owner unable to rent or sell the property. Fritz and I decided it was time to do an investigation into Foley Manor.

"Arriving at the house, I looked to Fritz's mustache for a sense of paranormal activity. Unfortunately, it was limp and unresponsive (not unlike Fritz himself). The next hour was spent searching the downstairs, but nothing could be found. As we proceeded to the upstairs, we heard strange sounds coming from a room at the far end of the hall. It was the young girl's bedroom. As Fritz cautiously entered the room, his mustache began to twitch wildly. There was a presence nearby. I whispered from the doorway for him to try to communicate with it. What follows is a transcript of the brief exchange captured by our digital voice recorder."

Fritz: Is there anyone here that wishes to communicate with us?

Spirit: (faintly) yes.

Fritz: Is that someone who would like to communicate?

Spirit: (a little louder) YES.

Fritz: Hello?

Spirit: (louder still) Hello?

Fritz: I can barely hear you. You'll have to speak up, please.

Spirit: Is this better?

Fritz: Not quite. Can you speak louder and more slowly?

Spirit: W-h-a-t-a-b-o-u-t-n-o-w?

Fritz: I can hear something, but it's muffled.

Spirit: I'm right here.

Fritz: It sounds like you're at the bottom of a well!

Spirit: Oh, forget it!

Fritz: I could almost make that out...Hello?

Spirit: You, sir, are an idiot!

GHOSTS & HAUNTINGS

Haunted Hole-in-One

If you're in the mood for good old-fashion fun (and perhaps a bout of stomach flu), you might want to check out Pirate Willie's Adventure Miniature Golf out on Route 9 near the Winchester Mill.

Locals claim the golf course is built over an old cemetery dating back to the town's origins. Reports say that when work began, bones were uncovered but quickly bulldozed over. The mayor at the time, William "Bill" McBeever, insisted nothing stand in the way of his dream: a pirate-themed miniature golf course. He would not get to see the park's grand opening, however, when he was mysteriously struck down with a severe case of diarrhea and forced into the hospital. The park opened as scheduled but was immediately befallen with strange events.

Visitors began to hear unsettling moans and see glowing apparitions hovering around the old shipwreck. Then people began to have a sick feeling suddenly come over them. At first the cause was attributed to Parrot Pete's Nachos from the snack bar. Claims of the cheese dip being left out quickly brought a visit from the health inspector. The nachos tested negative, but the cases continued, and the park was temporarily closed. The owners even invited local ghost hunters to search for the origin of the spooky activities. The information they received didn't take much of a rocket scientist to figure out. The spirits were definitely those of the town's early settlers. They didn't appreciate having their graves desecrated and were determined to make their point by driving everyone out. Despite this ominous warning, the owners decided to re-open the park, which was again plagued by the same gastric happenings.

Town officials now began calling for the park's permanent closure, but co-owners Ted and Beatrice McBeever (the mayor's brother and sister-in-law) remained adamant. They say that despite the boycott and declining attendance, they intend to keep the park open.

Ted defends the move, "We have a sign right at the front entrance that reads, 'Park may cause headache, upset stomach, diarrhea, swelling, dry mouth, difficulty breathing, disorientation, ghostly hallucinations, panic, outright mind-numbing terror, etc. Enter at your own risk!' We also ask everyone who enters to sign a waiver against taking possible legal action. We just want everyone to come in and have a great time!"

And what could be a better place for a great time than over the bones of the dearly departed.

Winthrop's

One of the town's oldest establishments is Winthrop's, located in the old VonHoudnas building. Winthrop's lunch counter has been serving its customers since the mid-1950s when it was part of the thriving business district. As the business hub shifted to the downtown, many of Winthrop's neighbor's soon departed, but the old diner stood firm. Today it may not be at the center of town, but it's at the center of many residents' hearts. The diner remains untouched by modernization, and everything from grilled cheese sandwiches to BLTs can be ordered off the original menu. It seems some things never change.

That could also be said of the numerous ghosts who are said to reside here. For years, customers have not only been coming to Winthrop's for the daily special but for the supernatural activity that is almost certain to occur. Far from being evil, these ghosts are quite friendly and only the least bit mischievous. When dining, it's not uncommon to see objects move or hear your name called out. And if you happen to catch a glimpse of a shadowy figure sitting at the counter next to you, don't be alarmed. It's probably just the spirit of Clem Hobtree. Although Clem rode off into the great beyond more than 13 years ago, he keeps coming back regularly for the patty melt.

Ginger Montegue, a waitress of seven years, describes her experience working here, "I've encountered all sorts of things. I had a cup of coffee slide down the counter by itself, which really unnerved me. I've also heard people talking and laughing when the place is completely empty. For awhile we had problems with the tip money disappearing off the counter. Once when this couple came in to investigate, they revealed that the person responsible was a former waitress named Ruby. They said her spirit was still here waiting on customers and going about her usual duties. Anyway, we worked it out so that me and the other waitresses all split our tips with her. Lord only knows what she needs money for, but I don't mind doing it if it keeps her happy. If she likes to work so much, maybe I can get her to work my weekends!"

The Phantom Flatulator

There's nothing particularly spooky or scary about this next story. It is, however, quite offensive. You see, the house at 2353 Jasper Park harbors an unholy odor, the likes of which might have risen from the very depths of the devil's own bathroom. Inspectors and fumigators of all kinds have been visiting the home since the smell began some 20-odd years ago. The septic tank has even been dug up and replaced three times to no avail. It seems no one can trace the smell to its origins.

Owner Gammy Johnson explains, "Sometimes you'll just be going through the house when suddenly you run smack dab across the most God-awful stench! It's like someone just messed their drawers. You know what I mean? Oh Lord! My dog wouldn't even stay in the house it was so bad. It was worse than cattle's business!"

Gammy has considered simply bulldozing the house down, but there is some public concern. For now the stench is safely behind the walls of the house. Some people fear that if the house is demolished the smell could get out and infect the whole town.

As councilman Harvey Laccardi notes, "We've talked it over, and I think for the time being we're going to leave the house just as it is. If you'll pardon the expression, we don't want to make a bigger stink of it."

Judge, Jury, and Barbecuer

In the town's long history, one name stands out as being the epitome of downright meanness: that name is Judge Jubal Duclaugh. During his 30-plus years on the bench, it is said he sent more men, women, and livestock to their deaths than anyone in the country. Boisterous and demanding, people feared meeting him on the street should they be accused of looking him in the eye or even, heaven forbid, breathing in the same air.

The judge was also well known for possessing a voracious appetite. Weighing in at nearly 300 pounds, he was never seen without a turkey leg or piece of pie in his pudgy hands. He loved food so much, in fact, that he had his own barbeque pit installed just outside his chambers. Anytime, day or night, it was said that he could be found grilling baby back ribs, a side of beef, or perhaps a whole hog or two. Lawyers often noted a trial would be put on hold while the judge tended to his basting and cooking. But in 1899, during a town festival, the judge's appetite would be his downfall. He had entered the chicken drumstick eating contest and was in the midst of a feeding frenzy, when he suddenly choked on a bone and died on the spot. As the townspeople gathered around his fallen body, many tears were shed. Tears of joy, that is. The people were so elated that after the judge's body was removed from the courthouse lawn, the festival continued for another three days.

Today workers say that although the judge may be long since departed, his spirit and appetite remains in the courthouse. A large black mass lumbering through the hallways is the most common incident reported. Workers also claim to have their packed lunches go missing and then later find crumbs littering the floor. Still others say they often hear a sizzling sound as if something is cooking and smell the heavy aroma of ham or bacon.

Luther DuWayne, a janitor at the courthouse for over six years explains, "Well, this place has always reeked of smoked barbeque. It's just something you have to get used to. They've tried every conceivable method to get rid of it, but as you know, the judge used to cook right outside there. I'll tell you one thing, haunted or not, this place sure does attract every dog and cat in the county."

The Touchy-Feely Ghost

The Clip 'n Snip Hair Salon is the site of our next story. Located in the old business district, this shop has seen its fair share of strange goings-on. Fire burned down the original building, a so-called "gentleman's club," in 1953. Several people perished in the blaze, which townsfolk claimed was God's retribution for the club's seedy dealings. A few years later a new building was erected, and immediately odd things began happening. People would report hearing noises such as laughter or whistling. One witness even claimed to hear a man's voice call out, "Let's have a look at yer knockers." Others would feel an eerie presence and then have the sensation of being touched- often inappropriately. Business after business tried to occupy the location, but the results were always the same. The building sat empty for more than 15 years before

beautician Margo de la Fontaine opened her shop in the late '80s.

Margo explains, "I had heard the rumors before I bought the place, but I've never been one to believe in all that stuff, so I figured I'd take my chances. I have to admit it only took a few weeks before weird things started happening: chairs moving, strange clouds of smoke appearing out of nowhere, and the image of a man appearing in one of our make-up mirrors.

"I decided to look deeper into the history of this place, and that's when I learned about the fire and the deaths of those men. Reports say it happened during one of the stage show performances. Some showgirl had lit her pasties on fire, and as she was twirling around, they flew off and ignited the stage curtains. I think the spirits that are here are those of the men who were watching the show. I've come to accept that. And usually they don't cause too much fuss. Sometimes you'll hear noises or feel something touchin' your hair. I can tolerate that. It's when they start playing grab-ass that I draw the line."

FOLKTALES & LEGENDS

Folks around here love to tell tales. It's part of the long (and some would say bizarre) history of Sleepytown folklore. The following stories are a few examples, as told by residents in their own words.

Hobo's Last Breath

There's supposed to be the spirit of a hobo in an alley near Main Street. Rumor has it that he froze to death one frigid winter night while trying to find shelter. Anyway, if you go down there at night, you're supposed to be able to see the hobo's spirit and maybe even his breath! It could be the middle of the summer, and people say you can see his breath as if it's freezing cold! I've gone down to the alley, though, and the only thing I've ever seen are two rats fighting over a piece of cheese.

Gramma with the Sharp Teeth

There's a tale about an old woman who was supposed to be a werewolf. One morning the woman's two grandchildren, a boy and a girl, came to her house and found her frantically searching for her false teeth. She asked if they would help her look for them, and they agreed. They searched the house high and low but couldn't seem to find them anywhere. Pretty soon the two children got tired of looking and decided to go outside. They were kicking a ball around the yard when the girl noticed a dead raccoon lying next to the sidewalk. Something shiny was beside it. Bending down to get a closer look, she saw a pair of dentures: false teeth with fangs and one single gold crown sparkling in the daylight. Quickly grabbing the teeth, she yelled to her brother, and they both ran inside.

"Gramma! Gramma! We found your sharp teef," they yelled.

"Well, bless your heart! You found them," the woman said as she gave them both a great big hug. "They were outside? I must have been sleepwalking last night," she chuckled. "You two deserve some homemade cookies for this. Would you like that?"

"Oh yes," they replied, their smiles exposing their little fangs.

If you Go Into the Woods Tonight, You're in Fur a Big Surprise

There was a family who was new to the community. They moved into a small house just outside of town with their two children and three cats. The first night in the home they were suddenly awakened by strange howling and rustling coming from the surrounding woods. The eerie sounds continued throughout the night until the sun came up the next morning. The same thing happened the second evening. The family was growing more terrified. On the third night, as the unnerving sounds began yet again, the husband jumped out of bed, grabbed his shotgun, and carefully crept out the backdoor. He followed the noises through the tree line into the dark woods. After walking only a couple hundred feet, he stopped cold in his tracks. Three huge forms were moving in his direction. In a moment of panic he charged into their midst and began firing away. When the smoke cleared and the screaming stopped, he realized he had mistakenly fired upon a group of rowdy lodge members. The Protective Order of the Sacred Squirrel was in the midst of their week-long ceremonies and dressed in full, fury regalia for initiation rites. Luckily, no one was injured. After hearing the man's story, the lodge members simply laughed off the incident. They promised to keep the noise down, and the man promised to put on pants before going outside.

The Man with One Boot

There used to be a really odd fellow who lived on the south side of town over by the railroad tracks. Although he was considered a recluse who never strayed far from his front yard, the man still attracted crowds of curious onlookers eager to serve witness to his strange behavior. Sometimes he would shuffle around his lawn at a snail's pace yelling, "Look at me go! I'm a cheetah!" Other times he might climb onto an old dog house and read aloud from a tattered notebook. He would ramble on for hours about only God knows what. The truth is, most of what he said was unintelligible gibberish. But what folks really got a kick out of was that regardless of the day or month, the man always wore a rubber galosh on his right foot (the left foot remained bare). There were many theories on the boot, but the general consensus was that the guy was simply off his rocker. It wasn't until after the man's death that a new rumor began circulating.

Upon examining the body, the coroner supposedly discovered the man's foot to be covered in thick yellow and white fur and had claws like a cat. Unfortunately, no pictures were taken, and no one else ever saw the extremity, but the coroner swears it was true.

To be honest, not much credence was given to the coroner's story. Most people chalked it up as yet another bizarre tale of a very strange man. However, a few still believe there might be some truth to the rumor. As one resident commented, "That was one strange dude. We always thought he might be on something, we just never figured it was catnip."

Horror d'oeuvre

My deceased mother-in-law Verona was a terrific cook but fiercely guarded the contents of her delicious recipes. She literally took them with her to the grave as a box containing all of her hand-written notes was placed beside her in the casket.

Several years later, we attempted to communicate with her during a séance. No one was getting a response, so I flippantly asked if she had any recipes to pass along. Immediately the psychic felt a surge of energy and began to scribble away on his notepad. As the information poured forth, the psychic could hardly keep up. When it was all over, a mish-mash of ingredients had appeared. It was a recipe, but a recipe for what?

Once at home, I couldn't wait to prepare the dish. As I studied the scribbled notes and measured the ingredients, I could hardly contain my excitement. Forty-five minutes later I was ready for tasting. Auuuuccck! Oh my God! That's disgusting!

The next morning I awoke in the bathroom, having spent a hellacious night sprawled over the toilet. I realized my mother-in-law was looking down on me having a good laugh.

No Nudes is Good Nudes

My grandpa once told me this story about a group of people who lived up in the hills. He said they were nudist hippies and would walk around, as he put it, "all free with the body." The townspeople just barely tolerated them because they mainly kept to themselves. One day, however, some of the men came into town sans clothes, and they were hanging out (literally) at the local tavern. The townsfolk were flabbergasted and went running to the sheriff. He told them not to worry, he would handle it. The crowd watched as the sheriff calmly entered the bar. Within seconds, the naked men burst out the door and ran as fast as they could back up into the hills never to be seen again. I asked my grandpa what the sheriff had said to make them leave. He said he couldn't remember exactly, but that it had something to do with mousetraps and hedge clippers.

Wanna Ride the Pony?

When I was about nine, I went with some friends to one of the yearly summer carnivals here in town. As we were wandering around looking at the sights, we saw this place giving pony rides. The kids looked like they were having a good time- the ponies, not so much. We stood there and watched a few minutes when suddenly I heard this voice call out, "Wanna ride the pony?" I looked through the crowd to see a tall, skinny man smoking a cigarette smiling back at me. For some reason, the sight of him standing there with most of his teeth missing struck me as funny, and I began to laugh. My friends were jabbing me asking me what I was laughing at. I pointed over at the railing, but when I looked again, he was gone. A bit confused, I approached the ride attendant. "Hey, Mister! Where's the tall guy that was just here?" The man turned to me and answered, "That's my brother Wilson." Then leaning in close he whispered, "Don't tell anyone, but he's dead." I felt a cold chill go through me. The man continued, "Yeah, he died here at the fairgrounds nearly eight years ago. It's nice, though, because I still get to see him. Plus, every morning when I come in, he's spent the night cleaning up all this straw and horse poop."

Ornamental, My Deer Watson

I heard this story from my cousin. He swears it's true. There was a house that had two plastic deer out front as lawn ornaments. The deer were kinda creepy-looking because they had huge painted white eyes with little tiny black dots. One night this man and woman, who only lived a few houses away, were passing by the house when they noticed the deer were missing. Just then they heard a commotion coming from the direction of their yard. As they slowly drove up, they couldn't believe their eyes. The deer were ALIVE and were trampling the heck out of the garden gnomes. The man honked the horn, startling the deer. He could see their crazy eyes illuminated by the headlights. They turned and bolted up the street.

The next morning the couple surveyed the damage. It was a shambles. Bits and pieces of the gnomes and their little village were scattered everywhere. Even the windmill was a goner. They looked down toward their neighbor's house, and there at the corner of the yard were the two plastic deer standing in their usual spot.

The couple was at home the next day when the doorbell rang. It was their neighbor who was warning everyone in the neighborhood about recent acts of vandalism. Someone was going around trashing and defacing lawn ornaments, and his two deer were victims; someone had cut off both of their heads. The man and woman said they had been hit too and would keep an eye out for any troublemakers. After the neighbor had gone, the couple returned to the family room to admire their newest additions. There, mounted on the wall were two plastic deer heads staring back at them with those crazy white eyes!

In the Still of the Night

When I was young, my siblings and I spent a lot of time at our grandparent's house. What we really loved to do was take our little suitcases over and stay the night. After a long day of playing games and eating candy, my grandma would tuck us into bed and tell us a bedtime story. I remember one particular story we always begged her to tell even though it scared us to death.

The tale was about an old woman who used to live on the spot where my grandparents lived. She was considered by many in the community to be a witch. People often reported strange activity coming from the shack where she practiced her black magic. After she died, it was said her spirit continued to be seen in the form of a glowing figure forever roaming the place where she had lived.

At this point, my grandmother would end the tale by saying, "So I don't want to catch any of you out of bed, or the witch might get you!" Nice one, Grandma. Most of the time we were so scared by what we had just heard that we spent the rest of the night wide-eyed and huddled under the blankets. But one time I got up in the middle of the night to go to the bathroom. As I was coming back to bed, I passed the upstairs hall window. I couldn't believe my eyes! There WAS something glowing outside moving slowly across the field. I stood there with my face pressed against the window, straining my eyes to get a better look, when my brother suddenly tapped my shoulder. I swear I jumped five feet in the air. As I turned back to look, the light was gone. My brother hadn't seen it, so I decided not to say anything to him or my grandparents.

Only later as an adult did I realize the story was true...somewhat. There actually was a glowing figure that could sometimes be seen walking in the darkness. The source of the light, however, was not a witch. It was, in fact, my grandmother. For many years my grandparents operated a still up in the wooded hills behind the house. Late at night my grandfather would sneak away to work on his prime moonshine. Then a few hours later my grandmother would go, lantern in hand, to check on him and bring him a late night snack.

Now, looking back on those overnight stays, things begin to make sense. Like why my grandfather often slept well into the afternoon or why Grandma always drank from a fruit jar.

The Wee Dandy Dublin

My Uncle Stew used to tell this old tale when I was growing up. It was about a little man who lived in a small field on the outskirts of town. Visitors to this area would report seeing a figure dressed in a frock coat, top hat, and short pants, dancing and skipping through the pasture. If he spotted you, he would drop his trousers, point to his manhood and ask, "Have you seen my wee dandy dublin?" He would then laugh hysterically and run off into the underbrush. Actually, now that I think about it, my uncle was drunk most of the time.

VonHoudnas

My great grandmother used to tell us kids this story when we were little. It always gave me the willies!

Back in the old days, Elwood Lambshire was one of the wealthiest men in the country. Recently widowed, he had arrived in Sleepytown and sunk vast amounts of his fortune into building what is now known as the "old downtown." His businesses included those for both the railroad and meat packing industries, which became so vital to the area during this period. Over a very short period of time, he became even richer. But by most accounts, Elwood remained a down-to-earth individual who didn't let his enormous wealth go to his head. He was quite normal except for one unsettlingly, bizarre thing. Elwood was never seen without his constant companion: a stuffed doll he called *VonHoudnas*.

The doll had been a mystery ever since Elwood first came to town. He carried it everywhere he went, whether it was in public, at work, or even church. Folks would often see Elwood behave as if in conversation with it, although the doll was never heard to utter a single word. There were also rumors that the doll would sometimes move its head or arms. The townsfolk were bewildered why a man of his prominent stature would display such ludicrous behavior.

One cool October evening, the truth about *VonHoudnas* was finally revealed. Elwood was attending an outdoor cookout at a local farm. The doll was, as usual, at his side. As Elwood passed the roaring campfire, he lost his balance and tripped. In an instant the doll went up in flames. People say the screams were ungodly, but they didn't come from the doll, they came from Elwood.

As it turned out, Elwood kept his entire fortune inside the doll. Every last dollar was crammed inside its pudgy frame. He was ruined. Eventually, Elwood was reduced to living on the streets, begging for change from passersby. And whenever someone would drop a coin or two into his tattered hat, he would utter a single word, "*VonHoudnas*."

MYSTERIOUS CREATURES

Lake Monster Makes for One
Pussycat of a Story

Lake Augustine. Folks who live around here call it one of the most beautiful spots in the entire county. Nestled in a valley surrounded by overlooking pines, the lake could not be a more picturesque or reclusive spot. But folks also claim it just might harbor a far darker mystery. Since visitors first started coming here to soak up the natural beauty and swim in the lake's cool waters, sightings of a large water creature dubbed Augie have been reported.

Throughout the years, several national groups have come to investigate the lake using a wide variety of methods and equipment. Unfortunately, not one was able to turn up any hard credible evidence. Now long since the last researchers have packed up and gone, one dedicated monster hunter remains: Junior Messencamp. Junior has been hunting the elusive serpent for the past year aboard his boat, the Augie Hunter.

"I was out here fishing one day by myself when I spotted something in the water," Junior recounts. "I saw this long neck rise up, turn toward me, and 'meow.' I swear this thing meowed at me like a darn pussycat. I shouldn't have said anything, but I told my wife. She just laughed at me and said I was drunk. Well, I couldn't get that creature out of my head. It was all I could think about. That's when I decided to quit my job, buy this old boat, and move out here."

Since becoming a full-time monster hunter, Junior only comes ashore to pick up a few groceries or meet with his wife and her attorney. "Yeah, Marlene is leavin' me. I guess all the suspense of me finding the creature is just too much for her to take."

As is the case with the most expeditions, the search for the truth is of the utmost importance. The tools used and the money spent can mean the difference between scientific justification or social ridicule. At the moment, Junior is facing the latter. Financially strapped and facing a mounting divorce, Junior has yet to put together anything resembling a serious investigation.

"Sure, I get laughed at most every day by the other boaters and fisherman," Junior explains. "I spent almost everything I had on this boat. I don't have all kinds of 'surfisticated parafernella' like them other guys, but I do have a few things. I've got this old tape recorder I found at a flea market. Now if I hear that meow again I'll be ready. I've also got my fishin' rod and net, a flashlight, and pocketknife. And I finally splurged and got one of those new underwater cameras. You can only use it once, but they're supposed to be the latest thing. I got it at the mini-mart the last time I went ashore."

When asked if he thinks he will ever find the elusive beast, Junior angrily responds, "Heck yeah, I'll find something! What do you think I'm out here all day long just sitting and waiting for? I just told you about my equipment! Why would I buy all that stuff if I didn't think there was something out here? I mean for God's sake, that camera cost eight bucks!"

Turkey Cobra

One of Sleepytown's oldest and most beloved mysteries involves the creature known as Turkey Cobra. The first mention of this elusive beast was on Halloween night, 1923, by a group of trick-or-treaters. The children claimed they saw the thing perched atop a fencepost, its freakish shape silhouetted against the moonlight. They gave it its unusual name because it had the body of a turkey and the head of a snake.

Locals speculated about what kind of animal it might be. Some thought the local fertilizer plant might be to blame. Contaminates in the soil could possibly have caused mutations in the wild turkey population surrounding Sleepytown. What of its unusually long neck? Could there have been some kind of bizarre turkey/snake breeding going on? No one wanted to go there.

Sightings and encounters continued over the years until the mid-'70s when the hysteria reached a fever pitch. Turkey Cobra mania was everywhere; kids began wearing Turkey Cobra t-shirts, restaurants advertised the "Turkey Cobra Lunch Special," the Turkey Cobra Disco step was even created by the local dance society. As often happened in the fad-driven '70s, however, the excitement died down, and soon the Turkey Cobra was back to being just your normal everyday mystery.

Possibly the last known sighting occurred in the summer of 1998 when two men reported spending an evening with the creature during an overnight camping trip. Claude Henry recounts the incident, "It was pretty late...after midnight, and we were sittin' by the fire drinkin'. We had pretty much been drinkin' all day. Anyway, I don't know how long it had been there, but we realized there was this 'thing' standin' between us. It was short with a round body and that real skinny neck. Maybe we shoulda' been scared, but we were so drunk I guess we didn't care. We just kept drinkin' and laughin', and the creature's head was bobbin' and swayin' like it was enjoyin' itself. But then Jim had to go and start tryin' to hug on it. Let me tell you, it didn't like that ONE bit! It started hissin' and flappin' its stubby wings. Feathers was flyin' everywhere. Jim had bruises from head to toe. The last thing we saw was it stumblin' off into the night. We prob'ly shoulda chased after it, but like I said before, we was drinkin'."

Fowl Weather

Reports of large winged creatures in the skies overhead have been plaguing the residents of Sleepytown for ages. People have claimed a multitude of terrifying personal experiences, such as near abductions and disturbing cattle mutilations, all attributed to the feathery beasts. Not surprisingly, these sightings have been occurring for hundreds of years dating back to the people native to this land. They called the creatures thunderbirds.

Today, people still report the occasional dark shadow passing overhead or terrifying screeching sounds from high in the trees. But now residents fear an even bigger threat from the mysterious creatures.

Resident Harland Sweetwater says he's not afraid of the creatures attacking him but more concerned with what they leave behind in their wake. "Just imagine getting up in the morning to find a huge mess all over your lawn. Most people say they want good solid evidence. Well, buddy. Here it is! I've got bird droppings the size of basketballs over here!"

One local shop owner claims the bird sightings have been good for business. He says whenever the reports start up, the customers simply flock in (no pun intended). "A lot of people are looking for ways to protect themselves against these flying creatures, whatever they are. They're really looking out for their own personal safety. That's why I try to keep my inventory of umbrellas fairly well stocked. They're great to huddle under from the overhead attack. Plus, when it's all over, you can just hose that sucker off!"

The Hairy Beast of Robey Woods

There have been sporadic reports of a hideous hairy beast seen in the woods surrounding Robey Lake, which is located just north of town. The beast is said to be over 6ft. tall, covered in thick fur, and smells, as one hunter claims, of cat urine and baloney. A recent eyewitness recounts that one foggy morning he came upon the creature near the riverbed. Rising up from a crouching position, it gave out a loud scream and jumped straight into the river. The hunter was so terrified he dropped his shotgun and ran like hell.

Town resident Jim "Jimmy" Buckwalter is a frequent camper to the woods but has yet to see the elusive beast. Mr. Buckwalter is a tall, burly man himself and could easily be mistaken for the creature. Asked if he is afraid of being shot, Jim responds, "I'm more 'fraid of the snappin' turtles when I'm in the river, to be honest. If there is a hairy beast, I ain't never seen it."

Some people say there's too much of a coincidence between the Hairy Beast sightings and Jimmy's camping excursions. They claim the creature resembles Mr. Buckwalter in more ways than one. Hunter Cecil Fletcher explains, "Jimmy Buckwalter is one hairy sonofabitch. He's covered head to toe with body hair. And now that I think about it, he does smell an awful lot like my cat. It wouldn't surprise me or anyone who knows him that he's out here buck-naked, skinny dipping, and frolicking around like an idiot. Let's just say, if I saw Jimmy naked, I'd run like hell, too!"

For now, the mystery will continue...

ACKNOWLEDGMENTS

I would like to thank my best friend and the love of my life, July, for her encouragement during this project. Despite my incessant ramblings about squirrels and ghosts, her support never wavered.

I would like to thank my brother Jeff for his incredible work on the CD. He has perfectly captured the personality and atmosphere of a certain sleepy little town.

I would like to thank my family and friends for their interest and encouragement during the writing of this project.

ABOUT THE AUTHOR

Mark A. Randall has always had a fascination with quirky characters and odd stories. Combining those elements with his love for history, rural America, the paranormal, and squirrels, "Welcome to Sleepytown" came to life. Mark grew up in a sleepy little town in Illinois and still calls the Midwest home.

LaVergne, TN USA
25 November 2009

165355LV00002B/65/P